蛾　　蜂

MOTH and WASP,

SOIL and OCEAN

土　　洋

Tilbury House Publishers
12 Starr Street
Thomaston, Maine 04861
800-582-1899 · www.tilburyhouse.com

Text © 2018 by Sigrid Schmalzer
Illustrations © 2018 by Melanie Linden Chan

Hardcover ISBN 978-088448-404-2
eBook ISBN 978-9-88448-600-8

33614080562837

First hardcover printing January 2018

15 16 17 18 19 20 XXX 10 9 8 7 6 5 4 3 2 1

Library of Congress Control Number: 2017952485

Cover and interior designed by Frame25 Productions
Printed in China through Four Colour Print Group, Louisville, KY

Dedications

To the memory of Pu Zhelong and the generations of farmers, technicians, and scientists he inspired. —S.S.

To my husband, Danny—my soil and my rock; and to my son, Eli—my ocean, my sun, my moon, my stars. —M.L.C.

Author's Acknowledgments

This book would not have been possible without the help of many people in China. I especially thank Gu Dexiang and Mai Baoxiang for their insights on Pu Zhelong's work and his interaction with villagers. Professor Gu was the original creator of the poem ("By day watch swallows on the wing ...") in the story. I am grateful to Chen Haidong, Luo Zhongbi, and others who shared their experiences as rural youth participating in insect control research. Although the narrator of this story is a fictional character, he is based on the knowledge I gained from speaking and corresponding with these thoughtful and generous people. I also thank Zuoyue Wang, Enhua Zhang, Zhang Li, and Cindy W. Chan for advice on how to balance art and precision in the book's use of Chinese characters. I am grateful to Karen Fisk for introducing the manuscript to Tilbury House, to Melanie Chan for her attention to detail and inspired artistry, and to our editor, Jonathan Eaton, for his extraordinary guidance and patience. The Eric Carle Museum of Picture Book Art has become a second home; Ferdinand and Anarres have deepened my love of picture books; and Winston has supported me at all turns.

MOTH and WASP, SOIL and OCEAN

Remembering Chinese Scientist
Pu Zhelong's Work for Sustainable Farming

SIGRID SCHMALZER

Illustrated by Melanie Linden Chan

TILBURY HOUSE PUBLISHERS, THOMASTON, MAINE

The first time I saw a scientist in my village was also the first time I saw a wasp hatch from a moth's egg. In that moment I could not have said which was the more unexpected—or the more miraculous.

It was the scientist, Pu Zhelong, who taught me that it was natural for a little wasp to hatch from a moth's egg ... and for a city-bred scientist, who had traveled across the ocean and back again, to get his legs muddy in the soil of the Chinese countryside.

My village is in the southern Chinese province of Guangdong. Today our region is famous for its blue-jeans factories, but when I was growing up in the 1960s and 1970s, most people were farmers. Every day my parents tended the fields. In good years the rice grew in long, golden tassels on the bright green plants, plenty to feed the whole village and to send to the cities as well.

In those days we were known for our lychee
orchards, too. Lychees are delicious.
When you peel away the scaly red
skin, the fruit inside looks like a
pearl, smells like perfume,
and tastes like
heaven.

Unfortunately, we weren't the only ones who loved to eat rice and lychees. Insects called stem borers hollowed out rice stalks, and the caterpillars of the leafroller moth withered the leaves. In a bad year, the scrawny plants gave us barely enough rice to feed ourselves, and none to send to the cities.

A leafroller moth lays eggs on a rice leaf.

A caterpillar hatched from an egg rolls one or more leaves and grows and pupates within, while the leaves wither.

Stinkbugs look like beetles and smell like farts. I don't know what they taste like, because I never wanted to eat one. A lychee that's been bitten by a stinkbug looks like a shriveled monkey head and smells bitter, and no one wants to eat those either.

We needed new knowledge to battle the pests. At that time in China there were few scientists, so kids like me were proud to go to the big school in town to study science. My mom was happy, too. She said, "With an education like that, you can get a good job in the city!"

But the village needed us, so after graduation we were sent home to experiment with new ways to protect our crops. The one I liked best was called the "lights of ten thousand families." Each evening at dusk, all the families in the village put out wooden dishes of water with kerosene lights. Insects would fly to the lights and drown in the water.

One year, we started using chemical pesticides. We felt very scientific when we carried the tanks on our backs and sprayed the crops with a long wand. The poisons sometimes made us sick, but we marveled at how we could kill all the bugs in just one day.

The next year, though, the sprays didn't work as well, and the year after that there were more bugs than ever. Each year we had to buy more of the expensive chemicals. Each year I felt a little sicker after I sprayed. And each year there were more bugs. My mom said, "The life of a farmer is too hard. A job in the city would be better!"

Arrival in Guangzhou
November 1949

JAPAN

CHINA

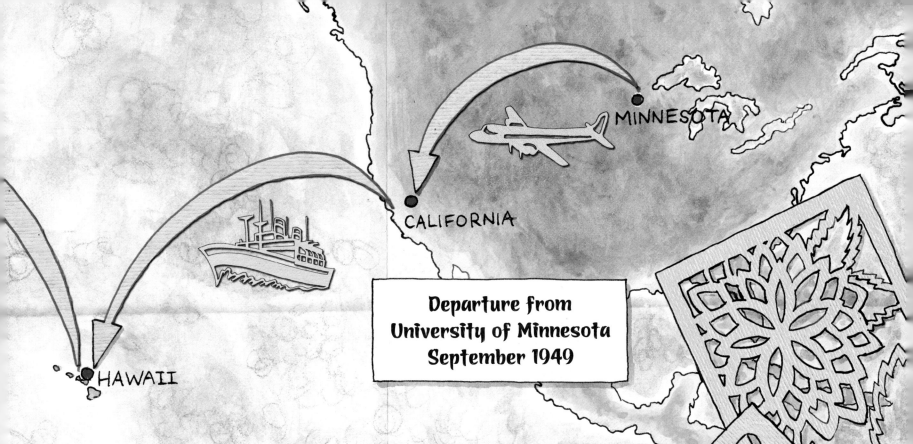

**Departure from
University of Minnesota
September 1949**

MINNESOTA

CALIFORNIA

HAWAII

Then one day we heard that an important scientist from a big university was coming to our village to study our insect problem. People said he worked in a fancy laboratory and had gone to school across the ocean in America. What would such a person think of our little village? Some of the kids from town looked down on their village schoolmates, calling us country bumpkins or muddy-legs. The scientist would be coming from Guangzhou, a big city with tall buildings and sidewalks crowded with people who never had to walk in the soil or work with a hoe.

With his big glasses and store-bought trousers, Professor Pu Zhelong looked very different from the farmers in our village, but he had a friendly face and a kind voice. He said, "You are not alone."

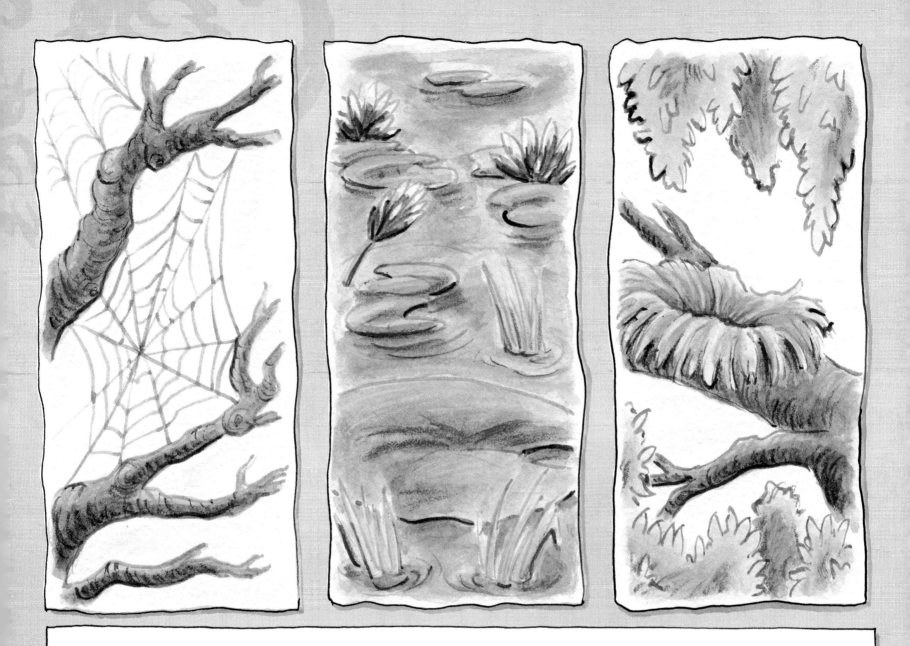

"When people in foreign countries started using these chemicals, they thought that the bugs would soon disappear forever," he told us. "They even collected specimens to put in museums! But instead, each year there were more bugs. The problem is that the sprays kill not only the pests but also the spiders, wasps, frogs, and even birds that eat the pests."

Professor Pu urged us to stop trying to kill all the bugs. Instead we should try to keep the numbers of all the different animals in balance. He taught us a rhyme to help us remember to protect the helpful animals:

By day watch swallows on the wing

In evening listen to frogs sing

While graceful webs the spiders string

I was dazzled by the scientist's words, but my father grumbled, "He's all talk. What does he know about farming? Those city hands of his are too clean!"

When the professor asked us to build a laboratory, some of the older villagers grumbled even more. "This means more work for us! We don't have money for his precious buildings!"

Then, the scientist from the city took off his shoes, planted a bare foot against a board, and picked up a saw. He didn't mind getting his hands or his feet dirty, and his kind of science didn't need any fancy equipment. Once we saw him with his shoes off, my friends and I quickly volunteered to help.

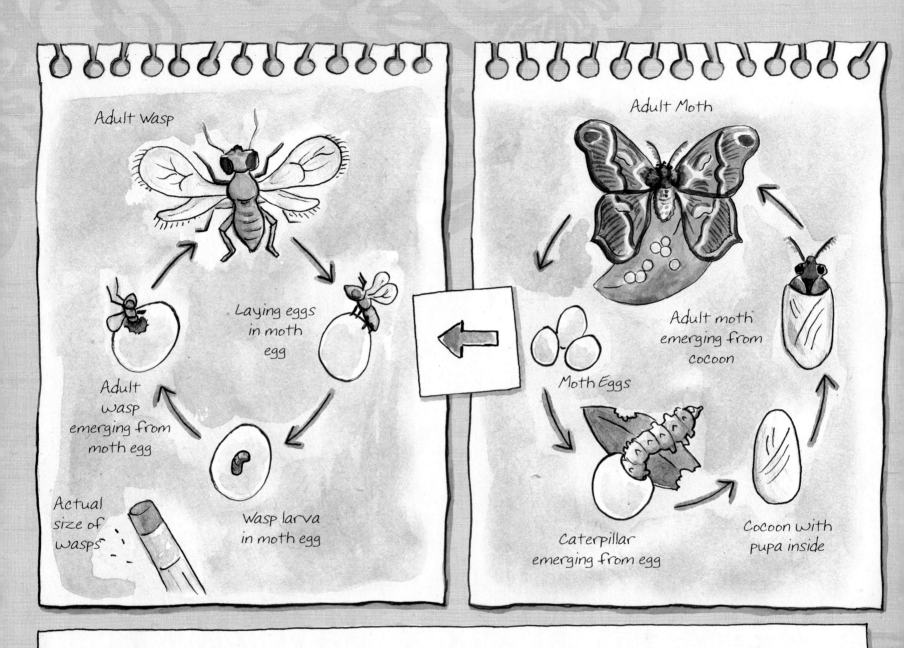

Adult Wasp

Laying eggs in moth egg

Adult Wasp emerging from moth egg

Actual size of wasps

Wasp larva in moth egg

Adult Moth

Adult moth emerging from cocoon

Moth Eggs

Caterpillar emerging from egg

Cocoon with pupa inside

Professor Pu told us about a kind of wasp that lays its tiny eggs inside other insect eggs. When the wasp larvae hatch, they eat the host eggs from the inside. The wasps were already living in our fields, but we needed more of them to eat the eggs of stem borers, leafrollers, and stinkbugs.

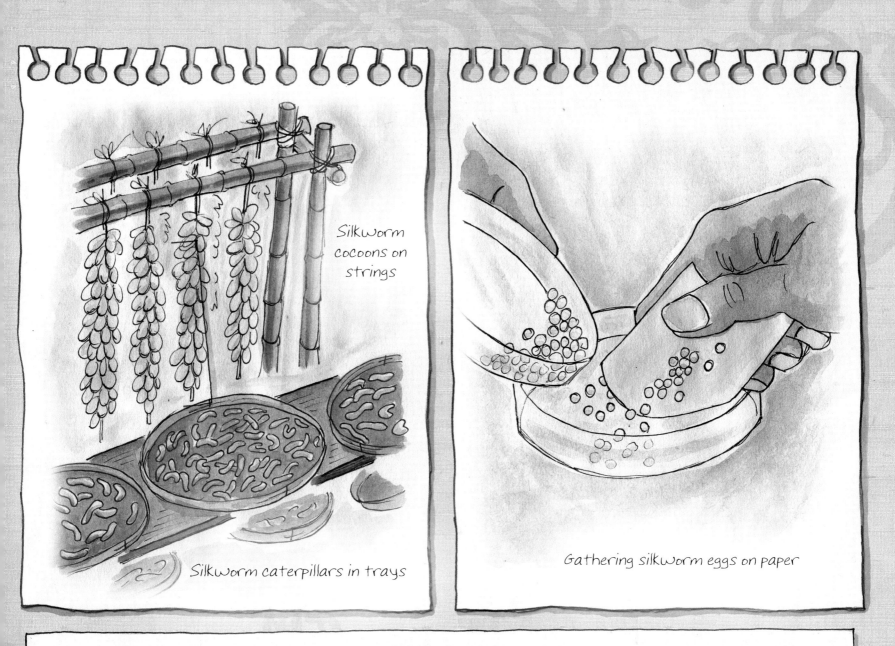

Silkworm cocoons on strings

Silkworm caterpillars in trays

Gathering silkworm eggs on paper

So we gathered silkworm caterpillars in trays made of reeds, and when the caterpillars spun their cocoons, we hung them on strings from the ceiling. When silk moths emerged from the cocoons, we put them in covered trays where they laid eggs. Every day we collected the eggs and glued them onto pieces of paper called egg cards.

Enlarged view of wasp emerging from silkworm egg

Silkworm egg cards in glass tubes
sealed with breathable fabric

Honey

Moth eggs in
matchbox

Enlarged view of wasp
larva and emerging adult

DOUBLE LANTERN

We put the egg cards into big glass tubes where captured wasps could lay their own
eggs inside the moth eggs. The wasp larvae hatched and ate inside the moth eggs,
and when they began to metamorphose into adult wasps, we removed the egg cards
and placed them into matchboxes.

Wasps among lychee fruit clusters

We put a bit of honey into each matchbox, then hung them among the lychee trees and in the rice paddies. When the adult wasps crawled out, they seemed to have hatched directly from the moth eggs! They ate a little honey and flew away to lay their own eggs inside the eggs of leafroller moths, stem borers, and stinkbugs.

Still, my father doubted that the wasps would solve our problem. "Those wasps are more likely to sting us than to bother the leafrollers and stinkbugs!" he said, and others agreed. Professor Pu understood. "A cautious farmer is a wise farmer," he said. "Until they've seen the proof, how can we expect them to believe it?" So he found a stinkbug egg, split it open, and used a magnifying glass to show them the little wasp growing inside the egg.

That year we used much less pesticide. Our village saved money, people didn't get sick, and our harvest was excellent. My father was happy; he didn't mind being wrong when there was more to eat!

Our village leader said that Professor Pu was a perfect example of what people in those years called "bringing together *soil* (土) and *ocean* (洋)." *Soil* meant local, rural, humble, and Chinese. *Ocean* meant foreign, modern, elite, and Western.

Scientists were expected to use what they had learned from foreign countries, but they were not supposed to stay in their university laboratories. They had to go out to the countryside to serve the people and to learn from Chinese farmers.

I began to think, if a scientist could come to the village, could a villager become a scientist? I decided I would try. I started by looking for something better than old matchboxes to house the wasps. I found little hollow bamboo stalks and cut them down to the right length. The professor praised my invention and promised to share it with others.

Bamboo vial with endcap

A few years later, my village supported me to go to college, so I went to Guangzhou to study insects with Professor Pu Zhelong. My mother was very proud: Finally I would have a good job in the city! An insect scientist cannot stay in the city, though. We must often go to the villages and work with farmers to protect the crops.

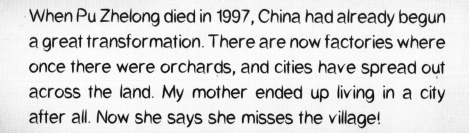

When Pu Zhelong died in 1997, China had already begun a great transformation. There are now factories where once there were orchards, and cities have spread out across the land. My mother ended up living in a city after all. Now she says she misses the village!

The problems with pesticides and other chemicals are worse than ever—in China and around the world. But there are many people working to find solutions. I am proud to carry on Pu Zhelong's work, bringing together soil and ocean—the Chinese countryside and the great sea of scientific knowledge.

Chinese Writing

Throughout this book, Melanie Linden Chan has incorporated Chinese writing characters in her decorative paper cuttings (a Chinese folk art) and in her narrative art. Modern Chinese speech and writing often use words of two or more characters to make meanings precise, but an object or concept can also be symbolized by a single character—with less precision but with more art. Melanie has chosen single characters for her paper cuttings. The Chinese characters in the book are as follows, with the pages on which they appear identified by the first line of text:

Title Page
蛾 (é) —*Moth*. In modern Chinese, we often call these 蛾子 (ézi) or 飞蛾 (fēi'é).

蜂 (fēng) —*Wasp*. This is a general term for wasps and bees. Honeybees are called 蜜蜂 (mìfēng). Parasitic wasps are called 寄生蜂 (jìshēngfēng).

土 (tǔ) and 洋 (yáng) —*Soil* and *Ocean*. Together, these two characters represent "native" and "foreign." In recent Chinese history, the combination has been used to symbolize the benefits of bringing together local, Chinese, or peasant knowledge (土) with foreign, university, or elite knowledge (洋). To speak more precisely about the soil or the ocean, we would usually use the terms 土壤 (tǔrǎng) for soil, and 海洋 (hǎiyáng) for ocean.

In those days we were known for our lychee orchards, too.
香 (xiāng) —*Fragrant*. This character is often used on its own to describe things with beautiful smells.

But we weren't the only ones who loved to eat rice and lychees.
虫 (chóng) —*Insect*. This character is also used for worms and some other animals. A more precise term for insect is 昆虫 (kūnchóng). Insect pests are specifically called 害虫 (hàichóng), meaning "harmful insects."

Stinkbugs look like beetles and smell like farts.
臭 (chòu) —*Stink*. This character is often used on its own to describe things with unpleasant smells. One word for stinkbug is 臭屁虫 (chòupìchóng), which literally means "stinky fart bugs."

We needed new knowledge to battle the pests.
灯 (dēng) —*Light*. Specifically, this character means the light from a lamp or other human-made source.

One year we started using chemical pesticides.
除害灭病 造福万代 (chúhài mièbìng, zàofú wàndài) —*Eliminating pests and exterminating disease will create good fortune for ten thousand generations*. Melanie recreated this image from an actual poster produced in China in 1960.

福 (fú) —*Good fortune*. This character is often used in Chinese art, including paper cuttings. Many Chinese families hang it on their doors for good luck.

With his big glasses and store-bought trousers, Professor Pu Zhelong looked very different from the farmers in our village.
平 (píng) —*Balance*. This character was originally created to look like a balance scale for weighing things. It can also mean level, calm, or peaceful (as in "peace": 和平, hépíng). A more precise term for "balance" is 平衡 (pínghéng), which is used in the term "ecological balance" (生态平衡, shēngtài pínghéng).

That year we used much less pesticide.
大米 (dàmǐ) —*Rice*. This is specifically the word for husked rice grains. When it is growing in paddies it is called 水稻 (shuǐdào), and when it has been boiled it is called 米饭 (mǐfàn).

获 (huò) —*Harvest*. This character can also mean gain or catch. A more precise term for harvest is 收获 (shōuhuò).

The History Behind the Story

Newspaper stories about China often focus on smoggy air, polluted water, and toxic chemicals. But Chinese people have played important roles in the efforts to solve these worldwide problems. This book shines a light on one such person, the insect scientist Pu Zhelong. (In Chinese, the family name comes first: Pu Zhelong's family name was Pu, and his given name was Zhelong, pronounced *Juh-lawng*, with the two syllables equally stressed.)

Pu Zhelong was born in 1912, the year China's last emperor gave up his throne. Over the next four decades, China was beset by many wars, and people in rural areas suffered terribly from hunger. Zhelong's family was well off and lived in the big city of Guangzhou, but when Zhelong traveled in the countryside, the contrast between the beautiful scenery and the hard life of the people there moved him deeply. In college he took classes in *entomology*, the study of insects. This fed his passion for learning about nature and gave him tools to control the insect pests that robbed farmers of their grain. And he met a young woman, Li Cuiying (pronounced *Lee Tsway-ying*), who was also studying entomology and who became his wife.

In 1946, with a civil war still raging and China's future uncertain, Zhelong boarded a ship that carried him across the Pacific Ocean so he could continue his studies at the University of Minnesota. Cuiying followed a year later. Zhelong concentrated on beetle taxonomy; he examined beetles found in China's forests and showed how they fit into the beetle family tree. Cuiying studied fruit flies.

On October 1, 1949, China's civil war finally ended with the Communists victorious. Many Chinese scientists living in foreign countries were afraid that the Communists would treat intellectuals badly, and they decided to stay abroad. But others, including Zhelong and Cuiying, were excited to return. They wanted to place their scientific knowledge in the service of the new nation.

The new government expected scientists to focus on practical subjects, so Zhelong stopped classifying beetles and Cuiying stopped dissecting fruit flies. They turned their attention to insect control again.

China was still a poor country, and chemical pesticides were expensive. Also, the new government's conflicts with the United States and other countries prevented China from importing enough chemicals. China had to find other ways to control insect pests.

And there were other problems with pesticides. They poisoned the environment and harmed people's health—and the insect pests soon adapted, so that more and more chemicals were needed each year to kill them. Many Americans learned of these problems in 1962 by reading Rachel Carson's book *Silent Spring*. All around the world, scientists like Pu Zhelong were raising the alarm.

Fortunately, there was already good research on *biological control*—using the natural enemies of insect pests to control their numbers. Pu Zhelong taught people to use less pesticide, and he found ways for villagers to raise and release large numbers of natural enemies, including parasitic wasps, bacteria, and even ducks.

The Chinese government supported Pu Zhelong's work and many other good projects, but it also supported the use of chemicals and encouraged people to kill sparrows and other animals that were important natural enemies of insect pests. Government policies led to even greater hunger than China had faced in the past.

Chinese scientists also suffered. The government often doubted the loyalty of scientists and criticized them for elitism—for failing to respect farmers and factory workers.

Sometimes scientists were punished, and some even died from their punishments. Things got bad enough that Pu Zhelong thought about retiring early, but he escaped the worst of those times and continued to do important work throughout his life.

The government wanted scientists to combine scientific knowledge with a humble attitude and a willingness to work side by side with villagers. This was called "bringing together ocean and soil." Professor Pu liked this idea. He had always respected villagers, giving them credit for the bamboo tube innovation described in this story. He especially enjoyed working with young villagers like the narrator in the story, who took part in China's "great agricultural scientific experiment movement," a program somewhat similar to 4-H. Not all young villagers went on to have careers in the sciences, but some did, and the luckiest had the chance to learn from great agricultural scientists like Pu Zhelong.

In the 1970s, the governments of China and the United States became friends again. After twenty-five years, Zhelong and Cuiying could return to Minnesota to see their old teachers and classmates, and they could visit other countries as well. But no matter how many oceans he traveled, Professor Pu never forgot the soil of the Chinese countryside. Until his death in 1997, he always kept his connections with villagers.

Today, pesticide use continues to grow in China, the U.S., and around the world. This has led to higher rates of cancer, ADHD, and other afflictions, and it has caused environmental damage including the collapse of honeybee colonies and losses of many other animals necessary to human survival.

But new generations of scientists are following in Pu Zhelong's footsteps. They can take inspiration from Professor Pu's deep respect for farmers, from his courage in the face of many obstacles, and above all from his commitment to finding environmentally sustainable ways to grow food.

SIGRID SCHMALZER, a mother of two and professor of history at the University of Massachusetts Amherst, has lived in China, holds a doctorate in modern Chinese history and science studies, and is the author of *Red Revolution, Green Revolution: Scientific Farming in Socialist China* (2016) and the award-winning *The People's Peking Man: Popular Science and Human Identity in Twentieth-Century China* (2008). This is her first children's book.

 Writer, artist, and new mom MELANIE LINDEN CHAN works in a variety of media—including watercolor, acrylic, and pen and ink—to create stories for children that open their minds to other cultures and ways of life. *Moth and Wasp, Soil and Ocean* is among her first book-length projects. Melanie researched her illustrations for this book with help from her husband's family, whose ancestral village, like the village in the story, is in the Pearl River Delta of Guangdong Province.

Further Exploration

Red Revolution, Green Revolution: Scientific Farming in Socialist China, Sigrid Schmalzer, 2016, University of Chicago Press. This adult-level book includes a chapter on Pu Zhelong that is his only English-language biographical treatment.

Bronze and Sunflower, Cao Wenxuan (translated by Helen Wang), 2015, Walker Books. A middle-grade novel on the joys and sorrows of the Chinese countryside during the Cultural Revolution.

Little White Duck: A Childhood in China, Na Liu (illustrated by Andrés Vera Martínez), 2012, Graphic Universe. An autobiographical graphic novel account of the author's childhood experiences in China of the late 1970s, with glimpses of urban/rural relations and children's participation in pest control campaigns.

Good Bugs for Your Garden, Allison Mia Starcher, 1995, Algonquin Books. A beautifully illustrated 72-page book on beneficial insects, including parasitic wasps. All ages.

One Good Apple: Growing Our Food for the Sake of the Earth, Catherine Paladino, 1999, Houghton Mifflin. A middle-grade book describing the problems of chemical pesticides and industrial agriculture and offering organic alternatives.

Rachel: The Story of Rachel Carson, Amy Ehrlich (illustrated by Wendell Minor), 2003, Silver Whistle / Harcourt. A picture-book portrait of the author of *Silent Spring*.

Silent Spring, Rachel Carson (illustrated by Lois and Louis Darling), 1962, Houghton Mifflin. The book that sounded the alarm about pesticide use in America and around the world. For middle grades and older.